THE GILDED AUCTION BLOCK

SHANE McCRAE

*

THE GILDED AUCTION BLOCK

FARRAR STRAUS GIROUX   NEW YORK

Farrar, Straus and Giroux
120 Broadway, New York 10271

Printed in the United States of America
Published in 2019 by Farrar, Straus and Giroux
First paperback edition, 2020

Illustrations by Christine Sajecki, using house
paint, india ink, and charcoal on Duralar.

The Library of Congress has cataloged the hardcover edition as follows:
Names: McCrae, Shane, 1975– author.
Title: The gilded auction block : poems / Shane McCrae.
Description: First edition. | New York : Farrar, Straus and Giroux, 2019.
Identifiers: LCCN 2018022909 | ISBN 9780374162252 (hardcover)
Classification: LCC PS3613.C385747 A6 2018 | DDC 811/.6—dc23
LC record available at https://lccn.loc.gov/2018022909

Paperback ISBN: 978-0-374-53871-2

Designed by Quemadura

Our books may be purchased in bulk for promotional, educational,
or business use. Please contact your local bookseller or the Macmillan
Corporate and Premium Sales Department at 1-800-221-7945, extension
5442, or by e-mail at MacmillanSpecialMarkets@macmillan.com.

www.fsgbooks.com
www.twitter.com/fsgbooks
www.facebook.com/fsgbooks

1 3 5 7 9 10 8 6 4 2

For Sylvia and Nicholas and Eden

Was it a whim of fortune,
Or was I hard to find?
What's the routine of a man with a gun?

Was it a kind of torture?
Have you been out of town?
What is it like to a man with a gun?

—STINA NORDENSTAM

What starts on the ground will end up
soaking into the ground forever.

—ANNE CARSON

CONTENTS

THE GILDED AUCTION BLOCK

THE PRESIDENT VISITS THE STORM

"What a crowd! What a turnout!"
—DONALD TRUMP, TO VICTIMS
OF HURRICANE HARVEY

America you're what a turnout great
Crowd a great crowd big   smiles America
The hurricane is everywhere   but here an
Important man is talking here   Ameri-
ca the important president is talking

And if the heavens open up the heavens
Open above the president   the heavens
Open to assume him bodily into heaven
As they have opened to assume great men
Who will come back   and bring the end with them

America he   trumpets the end   of your
Suffering both swan   and horseman trumpeting
From the back of the beast the fire and rose are one
On the president's bright head   the flames implanted
To make a gilded crown America

The hurricane is everywhere   but here
America a great man is a poison
That kills the sky the weather in the sky
For who America   can look above him
You're what a great a crowd big smiles the ratings

The body   of a storm is a man's body
It has an eye and everything in the eye
Is dead   a calm   man is a man who has
Let weakness overcome his urge for death
America the president is talking

You're what a great a turnout   you could be
Anywhere but your anywhere is here
And every inch   of the stadium except those
Feet occupied by the stage   after his speech will
Be used to shelter those displaced by the storm

Except those feet   occupied by the they're
Armed folks   police assigned to guard the stage
Which must remain in place for the duration
Of the hurricane except those feet   of dead
Unmarked space   called *The Safety Zone* between

Those officers and you   you must not vi-
olate *The Safety Zone* you must not leave
The Safety Zone the   president suggests
You find the edge   it's at a common   sense
Distance it is   farther than you can throw

A rock   no farther than a bullet flies

1

I FIGHT HIM (ANN PARKER)

I fell and broke   my arm some time ago
'Cause my right side am dead   and me
I tries to crawl   / Off'n the bed
I is a hundred three years old

When I gets back from the hospital
They ties me in this chair
I was a grown
Woman at the end of the war

The boy who helps me up and down
He wasn't raised like me he don't / Got the same manners
but   / We old ones know we still is got to be polite
To you white ladies

Daughter   did I tell you
My mammy Junny was a queen   in Africa
And I ain't had no daddy
'Cause queens don't marry yes   / She was a queen

And when she told them   at the farm

They bowed

She told them not to tell it tell   the master and they didn't tell

But when the white folks wasn't lookin'   / She was a queen

The boy   who ties and

Unties the rope he   / Says it don't matter who my mammy was

now that we's free

He fusses and I fight him and

he says a queen don't act that way

Daughter   you make sure you tell him

'Cause he don't know

And you don't know

A queen won't die a slave

EVERYTHING I KNOW
ABOUT BLACKNESS I LEARNED
FROM DONALD TRUMP

*"Frederick Douglass is an example of somebody who's done an
amazing job and is being recognized more and more, I notice."*
—DONALD TRUMP

America I was driving when I heard you
Had died I swerved into a ditch and wept
In the dream I dreamed unconscious in the ditch

America   I dreamed you climbed from the ditch
You must believe your body is and any
Body and stood beside the ditch for eight years

Thinking   except you didn't stand you right
Away lay down on your pale belly
And tried to claw your way back to the ditch

You right away began to wail   and weep
And gnash your teeth   my tears met yours in the ditch
America   they carry me downstream

A slave on the run from you   an Egyptian queen
And even in my dreams I'm in your dreams

BLACK JOE ARPAIO

America you wouldn't pardon me
Even if I was truly I was sorry
Even if I had worked so hard and truly
To keep the Mexicans   on the other side

Of the river   even if I had myself
Built turrets on a wall I built myself
Complete with searchlights and machine guns white
Men chewing toothpicks as they scanned the brown

Horizon   either through binoculars
Or aviator sunglasses the on-
ly sign of the expressions on their faces
Would be their teeth   you wouldn't pardon me

Even if I had   locked every freeway down
And every highway every street and road
And backroad every drive down   with police check-
points even if I had   made sure each cop wore his

No women aviator sunglasses
And mustache as he swept his flashlight first
Across your backseat then   across your feet
Then shone it in your eyes and asked for papers

Even if I had brought to life that dream
You at your bedside pray each night to have   A-
merica you wouldn't pardon me   I know
Whoever makes your dream   suffers your dream

DISPLAY FOOD

"We won with poorly educated. I love the poorly educated."
—DONALD TRUMP

America the lights along the highway
At night the streetlights look   just like the eyelets
At the edge of the tarp behind which Kim Jong-un
Himself detains the sun America
From you I drive beneath them seeking you

And in what other country   America
Could I within the country seek the country
And find it nowhere   but   the citizens are
Told   in the citizens the country fails
America I am becoming white

In the white light   in flashes   no one knows
And still for every inch my afro grows
I wait a minute longer at the Wal-
mart deli but I find   the real you there
Where what you see   will not be what you eat

SONNET FOR DESIREE FAIROOZ PROSECUTED FOR LAUGHING AT JEFF SESSIONS' CONFIRMATION HEARING

"Jeff Sessions' extensive record of treating all Americans equally under the law is clear and well-documented."

—SENATOR RICHARD SHELBY

America I'm laughing can you hear me
I'm laughing when I heard you say you   weren't
Racist because you shared a hotel room
On more than one occasion with a black

Lawyer I'm laughing while you worked to keep him
From voting   can you hear me when I heard
You say you liked the KKK   until
You learned the Knights smoke pot I'm laughing

America when I heard you say it was good
News for the South you *are* America
Good news for the South I'm laughing when I heard

You say that   after the Supreme Court broke
The Voting Rights Act please   tell it again
America   tell me the one I'm living

WE'LL GO NO MORE A ROVING

—GEORGE GORDON, LORD BYRON,
ALTHOUGH I FIRST ENCOUNTERED IT
IN A SETTING BY GEORGE WALKER,
THE FIRST BLACK COMPOSER TO WIN
THE PULITZER PRIZE FOR MUSIC

We'll go no more a roving from
Our bodies   love who once had roamed
So far as almost to have been
The owners of our bodies then

And not their property we'll   go
No more from the master's fields   and no
More love   we will we lay no more
The master's gaze and yoke we bear

Down in green grass that is grass green
The grass will take now   from our skin
Its colors and become us   love our
Browns will be all the Earth's wild colors

We'll go   no more a roving now
Except as the mule roves with the plow
The white stars make the endless black
A night   the master calls us back

AFTER CARRIE KINSEY'S LETTER
TO THEODORE ROOSEVELT

A colored man
came and he said he would
Take care of him
good care and pay me   five
Dollars a month his name is my
Brother he is
about fourteen years old his name is James

Robinson and the man who took him his
Name is Dan Cal
Five dollars for his labor his
Name is Dan Cal
I didn't know
The man before but now
I know him I has heard of him

From folks in town and from
elsewhere in the county in town
passing through
He sold my brother to

a white man named MacRee
They has been working him in prison for twelve month
And they won't send him back to me

he has
No mother and no father Mr. President they are
both dead   / I am his only friend
My brother have not done
Nothing for them to have him in
Chains and I saw no money
I believe Dan Cal lives high on it

He does if any colored man gets
money for   / A colored man's work
Mr. President but I will tell you I believe no
Colored man does   / Colored folks don't
make money we make food
For other folks to eat
And air for other folks to breathe

Excepting colored folks don't
make those things we are those things we are   food   we are air
I mend a white man's coat I am his coat
With every stitch I stitch my skin on tighter

Even when we sell ourselves
Colored   folks don't make money but we are white people's money
Dan Cal is a white man's dollar

By now my brother
is a pile of rocks
I know they got him breaking rocks
With every rock
He breaks he breaks himself
and he is more himself
Like he was always meant to be

that pile of rocks
But I'm afraid I wouldn't know him if I saw him now
I write for you to help me
I know you must be
Busy but it   / Wouldn't be nothing for you
Mr. President you
Are no one's dollar but your own

PURCHASE

America I was born incapable
Of owning what I work for   even   but
It doesn't   it never mattered doesn't mat-
ter where I went to school   or where I teach
Or who   America still my life belongs to
Somewhere a some white person who can't live it
Because I'm living it   America
And they would live it   better   easier

The way the maybe the   professor would
Or maybe he was staff   at Oberlin
The white man who   as I was walking to
Wearing a hoodie   to a meeting in
A building which was at the time a crew was
Repairing   he stepped up   to me and asked
So are you guys just drying out the floor here
How but with my life   can I answer him

Who calls me down from the gilded auction block

IF YOU SEE SOMETHING, SAY SOMETHING

"Congresswoman Maxine Waters, an extraordinarily low IQ person . . ."
—DONALD TRUMP

America I dreamed I looked at Auntie
Maxine and knew from looking   what she was
How smart she was   and also her whole fami-
ly what   they were and what they could be is

You my dream coming true America
No dream I've dreamed of you   would come true good
Though I have dreamed as good as you and you
Have often you have often told me dreamed

The best dream   for at least for almost one
Third of the declining years of your short life
You've often dreamed the best for me and mine
And I have seen your best and dreamed it of-

ten good   still in my dreams I see instead
Through the eyes you've placed in the back of my head

THE ROLE OF THE NEGRO
IN THE WORK OF ART

America I shower in the bright-
est bathroom in the house but it's the bathroom
With the lowest water pressure   most of the time
Your mighty rivers dribble down my chest   and
Back   in "The Dry   Salvages" T. S. El-
iot describes   "the river with its car-
go of dead negroes,   cows and chicken coops"
Because the river is   like time Ameri-
ca a   "destroyer" and "preserver" and
Like time America it's swollen with what
You eat   most   of the time   I don't feel like
I'm getting clean   your rivers dribble in
Bright light   preserver and destroyer when
I am seen how   will I survive being seen

THE BROWN HORSE ARIEL

Nigger-eye
Berries cast dark
Hooks—
—SYLVIA PLATH

Nigger-eye I   so dark when I was young
    I said to anyone and my-
self who would listen they were black   *black* black not
    Black like the pink of my pink palms

But black like no i-   ris all pupil black
    Black like you'd see a student who
Won't study like   I see you   riding by
    Sing-shouting *nigger-eye* and mak-

er I lament for thee and read thee still
    Black like the fear of death confounds me
Black like I named one black eye *Fear*   one *Death*
    Black like the brown horse Ariel

Who could not know himself   until he knew his rider

AFTER A PHOTOGRAPH OF A TOWN HOUSE IN THE LAFAYETTE PARK RESIDENTIAL DISTRICT DETROIT

Residents would be able, at [low] cost, to live in apartments and units designed by a leading architect and to walk th[r]ough a sylvan setting on their way to work in downtown Detroit. This not only promised to retain a middle-class population in the city but ridded the downtown area of slum-like housing and its black residents.
—CITY OF DETROIT HISTORIC
DESIGNATION BOARD

A giant   videotape a VHS
Cassette abandoned in a forest the
Flap broken off   the black   tape is exposed
And the brown trees turn black in it the tree

Barely a tree   nearest the tape and almost
But not   as tall the darkest tree   with the palest
Green leaves of all the trees the farthest from the
Lens of the camera   almost at the center

Of the picture its   trunk is so dark it dis-
appears in the tape the pale leaves seem to float
Although   the trunk is visible   in the pic-
ture in   front of the tape   where does the black

Body begin to disappear it dis-
appears   somewhere between itself   in the world and
Itself in the tape   so that it's not itself in
The tape   but void from which spring   the pale shoots

AWAITING THE GUNS

Daughter the drums and bagpipes pound and wail
And carry   across the only park you'll call
A park that isn't half   a swing set half

A jungle gym   and as I lean in close to
Buckle you in you   ask *What's   that* I glance through
The window just   behind your head and answer

It's just   musicians   then   I look again e-
ven though I saw I'm   certain   who knows when it
Comes when it comes   who knows who will be singing

GUNS WILL BE GUNS

"I can only say this: If [the man who shot the Sutherland Springs shooter] didn't have a gun, instead of having twenty-six dead, you would have had hundreds more dead. So that's the way I feel about it. [Gun control is] not going to help."
—DONALD TRUMP

America the guns themselves
if you   / Try to control them boy watch out the guns
Themselves will start / Killing
America they're very sensitive

America they boy   I'm telling you they want
They just want   to be held alright that's all they want
    America   who's
It gonna hurt   / Really
you might enjoy it   if you let yourself

America I wish it wasn't true   / And I don't
want   to have to say it but I do / Boy   I could say a lot of
    nasty things

But I'm / Gonna be nice
America   sometimes you have to just

lie back and close your eyes
lie back and close your eyes

2

REMEMBERING MY WHITE
GRANDMOTHER WHO LOVED ME
AND HATED EVERYBODY LIKE ME

America I was I think I was
Seven I think or anyway I prob-
ably was   nine   I anyway was nine

And riding in the back   seat of our tan
Datsun 210   which by the way Amer-
ica I can't believe   Datsun is just

Gone   anyway   America I was
Riding in the back   seat we were we my grand-
mother and I were passing the it must

Have been a mall   but I have tried   and can't
Remember any mall in Austin at
The time America but do I really

Remember Austin really   I remember
A thing that happened   once when I was passing
A mall in Austin so   a mall in Austin

But then and when   America will my
Grandmother be   my memories of her her-
self be   replaced by memories of just

Her presence near   important or unusu-
al   things that happened does that happen will
That happen   we   America we were

Anyway passing   on a city street
But next to it the   mall and actually
I must have been in the front seat actually

And maybe it was   winter all the windows
Were rolled up maybe or at least the one
Right next to me   in the front seat Amer-

ica when for   no reason I could see the
Window exploded   glass swallowed me   the way
A cloudburst swallows a car   glass and a

Great stillness   flying glass and stillness both
Together   then the stillness left   and I
Jumped either over my   seat or between

The seats   into the back America
Or neither here   I might just be remem-
bering the one real accident I've ever

Been in I was   a child still maybe eight
Or ten and we   were in an intersec-
tion hit   and I for sure jumped then my grand-

mother and I again already my
Memories of the Datsun breaking seem
More solid than my memories of her

But I remember her but all the feel-
ing   is gone from the memories but I
Remember accidents   and I remember

Silences after arguments but I
Remember her   teaching me how to hail
Hitler us shouting in the living room

And I remember   after the explosion
I said I saw a black man in the trees
In the bushes   on the traffic island with a

Black .45   I didn't I was lying
I think I was just trying   to convince my
Grandmother to   buy me a gun   for self-

Defense and for   in Texas even Austin
Self-definition   so I said I saw him
From the shadows   break the glass through which I saw him

FORGIVENESS GRIEF

Already what would kill you was
There   killing you   before you did
Those things that strip my memories
Of you   of love   already what

Would kill you was there   in the scans
Later I saw stained light how   hard
It was and is   still to accept
An innocent a physical   illness

As an excuse   I wanted you to
Have wounded me with your whole heart
As I had thought you loved me grand-

mother for what love ever have
I fought so fiercely   as I fought
To keep the harm you did to me

HATRED

I stood on the bridge in the sky   on the bridge between
Two buildings   at the second floor but in
Between the buildings so in neither one

But in the sky   at the second floor in the sky
Barely I had just barely   stepped from the
Nordstrom to cross to the food court barely   and I

Stood looking down   I stood still looking down
At the white boy with the Nazi armband on
Below me   to my right below then   I turned

And if I had fallen   straight down then he
Would have been standing right in front of me
He was beneath me   smoking talking we
Would have stood chest to back him   turned away

From me and to my right away   and smiling
Talking to the white girl leaning   against the wall her
Back against the wall him turning also

Sometimes away from her   and to her left
To blow his smoke away from her his   right
They stood so close together then they might

Have kissed   they didn't kiss   I watched   but they
Still might have loved each   other I watched   afraid
That if they loved each other I would see

SEAWHERE

America I am unnameable
Maybe you've never seen my skin my skin
Is brown but brown like   I might be Italian
Most often people think I'm Mexican

Once someone saw my double in Peru
She said *He had a noble soul*   I knew
Exactly what she meant   but smiled   Ameri-
ca now I might not have to smile   but this

Was 1995   and she meant well
I think   I am unnameable and so
I have no inner life no inner life
I recognize and so   I just don't know

Really what white   people are like inside
I know   better but worry the same goes for
Black people too   it was an accident I had
My childhood   black child raised by whites   and now

The problem isn't   that I don't see faces
Like mine it's that   I don't see inner lives
Like mine I mean the way   a person's inner
Life is expressed   partly by the public spaces

Created by their culture also   partly
By their behavior in those spaces I'm sub-
merged every day in the ocean of the inner
Lives of white people it's   white people mostly

To make my way through   you I have to borrow
An inner life   the way a scuba diver
Whose tank was empty might   borrow a mask
America   to make my way as Pharaoh

And Pharaoh's army made their way through the sea
Tell me where is the sea where   is the ocean
I cross to emigrate to you   I see
It nowhere   though it closes over me

IMMIGRANTS

My great-
Grandmother or
Her family was was some of them
Austrian some of them
Some German I imagined them
When I was young
Her parents meeting on a row-
boat in the middle of the Atlantic meeting they're
Escaping to America
They're wearing heavy woolen coats

They do not know   they will be hated in America

The ocean the
Atlantic clings   to them the
Cold spray the white fog clings
To them their   coats it seeps   into their coats   / And soon
    their coats
the heaviness of their coats
Feels like the heaviness
of   / Their own exhaustion soon
already   / There is no difference
Between the weight of their bodies
And the weight of the world

3

THE HELL POEM

Then Chukwu saw the people's souls in birds
Coming towards him like black spots off the sunset
To a place where there would be neither roosts nor trees
Nor any way back to the house of life.

     —SEAMUS HEANEY

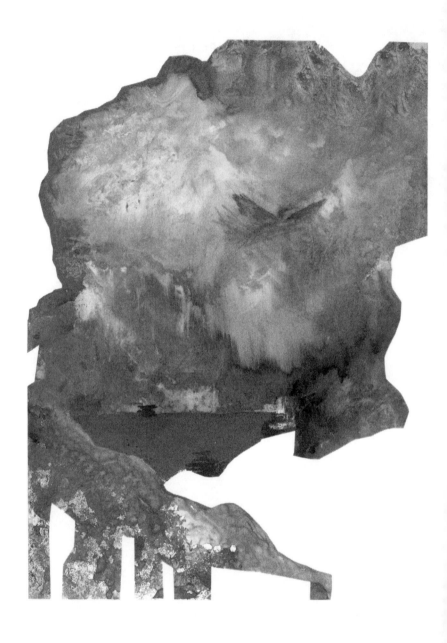

1. *Intake Interview*

Describe the lake I'm still
    not sure
        how I got here I was just hiking
        Or not exactly
    hiking but
I like to walk in the woods behind
My house I mean
    my apartment
        in the woods behind the complex so
        I'm hiking
    and it's a nice day a little
hot I guess but there's
A nice breeze so I'm hiking
    up this hill and I
        start to get really
        Hot and I
    can't breathe but I
just need maybe to rest for just
A minute so I look
    around for a bench or
        something but I can't

See anywhere to sit

and I have to sit or I

think   I'll faint

Then suddenly I'm rowing I'm

surrounded

by sailboats nice boats

Yachts I guess I mean

that's just a big boat

right white   yachts and sail-

boats and I'm rowing this

it's like an

open canoe   I'm rowing but

It's like I'm on a track

the waves don't

rock the canoe   and I stop rowing

But I don't slow down

plus I'm   invisible this yacht

it's drifting

It   looks like it's drifting slams

into me I mean   *BANG*

I thought

I was dead

but it bounces off I shout

but the passengers they all

Looked like that one

rich guy on *Gilligan's*

Island they don't   hear me they

Don't even flinch

it's like they're on   tracks on the yacht

it's like they're robots

At Chuck E. Cheese and

me it's like

I'm in a bubble on a track

Too I'm   fine

I don't feel a thing

so now of course I'm terrified

Describe   the bird the bird

the bird

looked like a big   gray seagull but

The bird looked like a robot too

but free   the bird looked free

it dove

And landed in the boat at my

feet in-between my feet

and spoke

It sounded like a dog

barking it

sounded like it couldn't speak

It said

barking it said *Hey   fuck you*

asshole you fucking asshole fuck

You follow me and coughed this little

skeleton hand up

middle finger up

Then it took off

barking

the bird looked free it couldn't have

Been free   if I was stuck

and followed it

stuck on a track   or maybe

It was free but everybody

has a boss

I let the oars slip

Into the lake

except they didn't

sink they just stood there   then heads

And necks and faces

sprouted from the handles then

arms and legs sprouted

From the sides   and the oars walked away *Describe*

the oars

the oars   walked on water

Like oars
their faces steamed in the sun
and the steam caught the light from the sun
And glowed above their heads they
walked   away
from where the boat was going
Describe the gate the boat kept going
toward this weird
whirlpool in the middle
Of the lake it was
I mean the water looked
pixelated white but splotchy
And the water   twisted
pixel   by pixel
from pixel to pixel
It looked like it would hurt to fall in
the pixels looked
well   square   but sharp and
That's where the boat
took me the whirlpool
chewed the boat   to splinters   and
As the boat broke
and sank I looked
down   and saw I was floating level

With the surface of the lake

and the lake

on all sides was rolling away

From me and I saw night

beneath me

and for a moment I was   any-

one watching from   above me would have

seen a bright spot

in a big darkness

I must have been

I must have looked

exactly like   if only then

The man I always thought I was

floating above Hell

and then I fell

2a. The Fall | The Tyrant Beetle at the Banks of the Living River of the Dead

I fell a whole   lifetime of fall-
ing as I fell   and as I fell I
Fell through my life I watched my life

Projected   on the walls of the hole
I fell through but projected through
No lens no carried by no light

No but projected   like a movie
On the walls of the hole I fell through but
Backward like   watching was like watching

A movie from behind the screen
In kind of it was   in black and white   but
In supersaturated whites

And blacks like scraps   of carbon paper
Their edges spilling over the edges
Of the darknesses in the world the blacks and

Whites overflowed the objects they
Belonged to the objects   I had thought
Belonged to them   and as I watched

Falling   the camera overflowed
The edges of my memories
Once   and again and then again

To follow people I had hurt
Through selfishness   through inattention
From the edges of my memories

Into their memories and lives
I saw the harm I did   I saw
Eventually I   even my

Harm   disappeared I disappeared I
Had thought   at least the scars I made
Would be the scars I made forever

I was a desk lamp next   to shadows
That would not be if it were not
And are its children and itself

And fade when sunlight fills the room
As I fell   slow through darkness watching
Memories carried by no light

Until I didn't I   just   stopped
Falling suddenly and no impact
Suddenly I'm   standing in
A room my back against   it feels
Like skin a wall but   only as long as
It takes for me to realize
I'm standing in a room my back
Against a wall   and the wall oppo-
site from me disappears the wall
Behind me slides   forward and shoves
Me out I stumble into a
Cave or a warehouse somewhere big
And dark that didn't really feel like
Part of the world   facing a row
Of mumbling kneeling   corpses their
Eyes open their mouths   closed but mumbl-
ing but their voices didn't   the
Sounds of their voices didn't come
From them their voices   flooded from
A giant black   hundred-legged beetle

Hovering in front of and above
The corpses its black back to me its
Pale orange belly   pulsing a
Different voice   pouring from each leg and
As I stepped near   it spoke to me
But somehow only in my head
Look at me   I'm a huge   success   you
Want to know how I got to be where
I am   of course you do   of course
You do   see this   tremendous line
Of people here   I promise you
Trust me   ok   you will not find
A more tremendous group of people
Anywhere   ok   and they're all waiting
For me   just to hear what I'll say
Ok   and they don't know   can you
Believe it   they've already heard it
You're hearing it right now   believe me
It might not sound like much   but when
I'm all you hear   and all you see
I'm everything the beetle's voice
Swallowed my mind consumed me I
Staggered to one   end of the row
And knelt and as I knelt a man

At the other   end of the row stood
And walked   into the dark beyond it
Opening and closing his
Mouth   like a goldfish what   I think
Breathing   or like a cartoon shark
Chasing a goldfish really just
Snapping its jaws its fat shark head
Stuck in the bowl   and disappeared
Into the dark beyond the corpses
Talking   out loud his body dis-
appeared   but as his body faded
His voice detached from the beetle and
Became his voice again which I
Had never known to be his voice
And as his body disappeared
His voice grew stronger and I heard
Him call my name   and stood   my voice
By then had nearly left my thoughts
As when a cartoon scientist must
Enter a sick friend's body in
A specially built submarine
That shrinks and is herself shrunk down
To microscopic size her voice
Shrinks and becomes a squeaking noise my

Voice had become a squeaking noise
Behind the sniffing   wheedling noise
That was the beetle's   actual voice

I stood   and staggered into the
Darkness beyond the corpses   there I
Saw the man who   had risen and walked
And who as waves   are freed and roll
Across a tub   only to break
Against the belly of the man
Who freed them climbing in   the man who
Had risen was free   only to walk
From one oblivion to another
From noise to all I saw   was empty
Darkness   and I followed him
But caught him only after we
Had walked too far to hear the voices
Although the beetle's orange belly
Still pulsed in the distance like a turning
Lighthouse beam   or a house burning
On a far shore   the moment we
Stepped beyond the noise horizon
The man stopped short   I following
Too close and reaching   out just then

To tap his shoulder stumbled and
Fell into him   and the man fell
First to his knees then   forward onto
His face without   raising his arms
To stop himself   among the dead I
Mistook the dead for the living and
Afraid he might be hurt   I crouched
And rolled him over   and he spoke then
I didn't   call your name I just
Said it out loud I just   it had
Become my name the moment you
Knelt I just   wanted to hear it
I wasn't   asking you to follow
Me   the river   was the river
Lethe the dead forget their lives there
As eddies in the ever-changing
Living river of the dead   I
Left it to find my Hell   I don't
Know what I did to earn my place
In Hell   I took your name   as mine
Was taken long before you came
I couldn't   when my name was taken
I couldn't rise to follow it
How did you rise to follow me

Before I had a chance to answer
I heard the sound of hammers striking
Metal and raised   my eyes to look
And in the once-empty darkness there
Before us now I saw a huge
White factory and floodlights most
Trained on the factory and one
Sweeping the field surrounding it
And in that light the man who fell
Vanished he vanished as the beam
Swept the black ground before me asking
Again *How did you rise*   the beam
Swept past me stopped   swept back and stopped and
Fixed on me   first yellow   then orange
Then red then light and heat combined
The heat that had been   weaker than the
Light when the light was orange now was
Equal to the light the red light dimmed and
The heat increased the factory's
Enormous rolling door rolled open

2b. The Angel of the Body

And two human-   shaped shapes emerged
From the dark inside   and called my name

I almost didn't answer them
I turned   but found the field behind
Me gone I found a wall behind me
Cinder block   painted red   it rose
Into the sky   by which I mean
It rose to where if there had been a
Sky the sky would have been   and past
Where the sky would have ended I
Swallowed I   tasted blood   I answered
The hammers stopped   the red wall dis-
appeared a high-pitched *Whoop Whoop Whoop*
Rushed I turned back to look   from the fac-
tory I couldn't see the source
I ran   my footfalls echoed first
One echo for each footfall then
A second then a third the echoes
Slipping out   of phase with the sounds
I made   and overhead I heard
Wingbeats and *Whoop Whoop Whoop* the light
From the beetle's belly as I got
Closer retreated as I got

Closer the light   changed from orange
To red and as the light retreated
The heat increased   until the light
Was a small dot on the horizon
And the heat was unbearable

And then the echoes stopped   and I
Stopped running *You   don't choose to run*
I choose to make you run it was
A small child's voice behind me shouting
I choose to drive you closer to
The fire you hope will rescue you
The wings you heard were my wings beating
The feet you heard were my feet running
I am a many in a one
Hunting I join the sky to the earth
As hunting I join life to death
And stand between them   like a dam
Between a river and a lake
I called your name from the gate of the city
I   was chasing you before
You answered turn   and face me   yes
Why do you cringe and cower aren't
You dead   already aren't you damned
Already but   perhaps you still
Love that   trophy you call your body
You can't   love it here you   can't own it

Here   and what else has your love been
What hasn't your love claimed   you need-
n't fear   to lose that love you will
Lose nothing but the great delusion
That brought you here   you will be free
At last you won't be   subject to the
Whims of that   body   which because
You didn't recognize it was
A mind was stronger than your mind
Be glad   here   let me help you root
Your love out   have you felt around
For it I'll show you   where to look the

Demon   who had spoken from behind
Me before   now rose from the dirt
In front of me four   legs four arms
Four wings   two heads the same   child's face twice
And twenty fingers   twenty claws
They plowed a claw across my chest
And reached inside the   robot bird
Alighted then   on the demon's shoulder

And as my vision darkened as I
Lost consciousness   spat   and barked *You're*
So fucking stupid I can't stand it

At that a darkness like the darkness
Before the world was overtook me

2c. A Glimpse of the Burning Edge of Heaven

I dreamed I was alive I dreamed
In Hell I woke dreamed waking on
A mountainside   I dreamed I woke
But in the dream I also dreamed I
Had been awake   for years on the mountain
I dreamed the bird had brought me there
I dreamed the bird had carried me
To the mountain from   between my first
Death and a second death it said
It couldn't stand to watch I dreamed
I rested on the mountainside
Cross-legged and   for years the bird
Had come and gone   many times come
And gone and it had mentioned many
Times a test I might   not recog-
nizing it fail   and though the bird had
Threatened and tried   to bribe me with
More life I hadn't risen   at
Those times I watched   pine trees at the foot
Of the mountain inch   toward the mountain
Then back again each breathing and

Breathed by the mountain every living

Thing on the mountain   moved as if

Breathed by the mountain   in and out

I saw more clearly as I rested

Everything moving   back and forth

Until the sun itself as slowly

As it moved   seemed to be a part

Of the motion   in and out   and back

And forth   so that I saw it even

In the night   moving on the other side

Of the world so that I saw the darkness

Deepening as the sun drew closer

To the spot on the other side

Of the world   farthest from the mountain

And from the moment the sun left

That spot I saw the morning coming

In the changing blackness of the sky

For years I sat on the mountainside

And watched the bird fly silently

Across the sky   from south to north

Or what I thought was south to north

And as it always   as it flew

To the north it crossed between the sun

And me at the zenith of the course
Of the sun across the sky   and al-
ways as it flew to the south it crossed
My zenith just   as the sun disap-
peared over the horizon for
Years I watched and after years
I saw the bird begin to change
I saw the bird begin to fade
I saw and watched it   silently
At first the bird   looked like an image
Moving across an image burned
Into a monitor   but soon
The bird looked   like an image burned
Into a monitor   but moving
Behind the image in the foreground
And then as I was watching it
One afternoon or morning as
It crossed the sun the sunlight burning
Through it I   was blinded for
A moment   and when I could see
Again the bird was gone   I searched
The sky   and searching realized
The sun was still   the distant clouds
Were still and I glanced down and saw

Only the pines at the foot of the mountain
Moving the pines at the foot of the mountain
Began to climb toward me

                      I dreamed
They climbed   faster than any living
Being could climb   as if they were
Not bound by life to the world they lived in
And darkened as they climbed   and their
Dark needles as they climbed glowed   red
And redder and   when they had almost
Reached me the bird emerged from them
And flew ahead   and turned its back to
Me and the bird spoke then   to the pines

It spoke a language I had never
Heard it sounded speaking like
Wind in pine needles the trees spoke back
They spoke   a different language back
Their language sounded like a bird's
Wings flapping as it leaves a tree
But I could see they understood
Each other and   the pines stopped climbing
Their needles faded   they turned back

And climbed down slowly the bird watched
Them silently they made it half-
way back   down to the foot of the mountain

Then   the dream changed the sun slipped down
To the edge of the sky the sky itself
Even before the sun set went
Black and the pines ignited burn-
ing needles flew   from the pines in all
Directions the   pines burning looked like
Sparklers throwing off slow wander-
ing sparks then   the sky opened as
The sky would open or a U
FO would open in the sky
To take a soul   to take a person
Away   but all it took was fire
The flames grew taller seemed to stretch
Taller to reach the hole in the sky
They rose   and rising they released the
Pines and the pines stood   dead on the mountain
The bird   who had until now watched them
Shifting its weight   from foot to foot
Now turned to me   and barking asked
Why fucking don't you fucking   go   oh

Shit   shit I've seen that look before
Shit even this   even   Hell you think it's
OK   shit   you   you know   I've been
Watching you since before you fucks
Knew you were you   you know what makes you
Monsters   a human is the on-
ly   creature that can fatten con-
suming itself it's Hell it's fucking
HELL and the bird it was   shaking lunged
At me it tried to lunge but could-
n't but it   as if it were chained
At the ankle to a peg in the dirt
Snapped back and almost   fell and then
Shaking it tried   to fly it leapt
Flapping its wings they sounded like
Chains rattling the bird fell face down
In the dirt hot light   burst from its back that
Light not the melting bird's   screams   woke me
That sounded like a world of screams
I heard the world   and still I dreamed

3. A Face

I woke in light in dirt
In a road   healed in what
Looked like an old west ghost town
The kneeling corpses kneeling

At the edge of the town
Facing away   the robot
Bird circled overhead
Then seeing I had woken

Landed beside me opened
Its gray beak wide   and barked
And spoke   *Before am was*
I am   and sought to be

I am and seek to be
And seeking I made you
And all your kind   your kind
My child   for surely mine

My child   for surely mine
My child Hold on a sec
This fucking thing   it always
Sticks fuck him the useless

                    Fuck and the robot bird
              Unfurled its metal wings
Took off   and threw itself
Into a pillar growling

                    That ought to   fucking do
              It then   the other voice
The human voice inside
The robot bird's breast shouted

                    MY CHILD   *for surely mine*
              Best born if not the first
You are   Death came before
And bears the imperfections

                    Of a first draft my   child
              I seek and I have sought
From the beginning to
Help you to grow   if I

Have not seemed nurturing
Know I have striven none-
theless to attend to our
Relationship and would

Not choose if I could choose
To be ignored   love binds us
Through   I acknowledge   in-
termediaries but

The more tangled the knot the
Stronger it holds   beloved
I welcome you to Hell
As a new mother welcomes

Her child to its life and body
And fear I must apol-
ogize for both   I made
You what you are   death-seeking

Out of pity for
My son   Death   who before
You couldn't find a job
But surely there are worse

Reasons for being   haven't
You often wished you knew
Whether you were conceived with
Love   for love's need   you were

My child you were   and serve
A purpose   you are Hell
Its living walls   its rivers
You are each other's flames

In life and in this life
And you will find yourself
Unchanged   but would you know
Yourself if you weren't burning

I see your crime was love
You loved the world   and wanted
That love to end your ob-
ligations to the world

Why make the world   a garden
If you would punish its
Keeper for loving it   as
A father loves his wife

Here you will   be the world I

Grant you a part in it

Forever   I grant my wish

For you   to you   at last

You are what you were made for

And more so what you make

Employment and a home

For the god at the end of the world

Then the bird closed its beak

And turned its back to me and

Darkness spread across the

Ceiling   but the bird didn't

Leave   but turned back to me

And barked *Same speech   for I*

Don't fucking know how long

Five thousand years   I mean

Five thousand years ago   sure

Death was the god at the end

Of the world   but now   nah   now

Death's just the caterer

After a big-ass party

No   it's you shits now

You know   the boss was there

At the beginning of

The world you want to know what

God said   what words God spoke to

Call humans into being

The boss says God said Snails

Make shells   humans make hells

And winked and there you were

And there was Hell beneath you

A face beneath a heel

But the boss lies a lot

Then   the bird turned again

And flew   toward the dark

Ceiling and even   as it

Filled the darkness   it dis-

appeared in the darkness   like

Paper burned loose from the kindling

And flying from the fire

4

THE MONSTER MADE OF AMERICA
DREAMS OF AMERICA

I'm made of murderers I'm made
Of nobodies and immigrants and the poor

and a whole   / Family the mother's
liver and her lungs

and the left half of the baby's face
The doctor   / Stitched it to the right half of the father's face

So that the smaller face
would pull the larger up

He said he thought
I would look happy but I see them   / In the mirror every

Morning I have to even
I   in the morning have to   look I see them

staring at each other
not of   / Course with their eyes

but such   true and such deep
Revulsion shapes the whole expression they

Stare with their foreheads with their mouths
Their noses and their cheeks   / They stare   and each

Struggles to push itself away from the other
Even when they're calm they ripple at their edges   / Like water
     just before it boils

None of this hurts
Not in the way you might expect

But still I can't get used to it
And in the gap that opens if we ever

Meet   don't be frightened
It never opens very wide

I don't see blood I don't see / The pulpy
white skin beneath skin or even

The skull itself half   / A baby's skull and half a grown man's
but a different baby and a different man

I see green grass
A row of blades laid flat and close

My fingers are too fat
to fit inside the gap

But I have almost worked the courage up
To pry it   open with the crowbar / The doctor

Dropped when he fled
I think I will find earth beneath the grass

AFTER THE SKINNY REPEAL
IS VOTED DOWN

Even if only   as one breath they
Something of them   will help my daughter's
Child if she chooses   to have a child to
Be whole   even as ash   in the wind then
In a dark cloud   then in the rain then
In a bright cloud-white blossom blossom-
ing then   in the ripe fruit   then cold in
Cold orange juice in a white cup the
Four strangers at   a Wendy's at a
Table across the room   I hear them
Talking about their children's children
That one is doing better now in
School and what made the difference and
Whether one really should have gotten
A car for Christmas   as around us
Clear windows are obscured by clear rain
I breathe the words they say to each other
We live and die apart together

NOTES

ACKNOWLEDGMENTS

NOTES

"I Fight Him (Ann Parker)" is partially adapted from an interview with a former slave named Ann Parker, which was conducted by Mary A. Hicks, an employee of the Federal Writers' Project, in the 1930s.

"After Carrie Kinsey's Letter to Theodore Roosevelt" is partially adapted from a letter Carrie Kinsey of Bainbridge, Georgia, sent to President Theodore Roosevelt on July 26, 1903.

The phrase "the fear of death confounds me," in "The Brown Horse Ariel," is a translation of "timor mortis conturbat me" from William Dunbar's great poem "Lament for the Makaris."

The photograph referred to in "After a Photograph of a Town House in the Lafayette Park Residential District Detroit" was taken by Michelle and Chris Gerard.

The visual pieces accompanying "The Hell Poem" were all made by Christine Sajecki. Find more of her work at christinesajecki.com.

ACKNOWLEDGMENTS

Special thanks forever to Christine Sajecki for her beautiful paintings and for her friendship. Thanks to Melissa McCrae for her patience, and love, and patience. Thanks to Dan Chaon, Jonathan Galassi, Garth Greenwell, Derek Gromadzki, Suzanna Tamminen, and G. C. Waldrep for helping me to figure out this book, as well as for their friendship. Thanks to Sean Shearer at *BOAAT* for allowing parts of "The Hell Poem" to be reprinted by *LVNG Magazine*. And thanks to the editors and staffs of the following journals, in which earlier versions of these poems first appeared:

The Believer: "After the Skinny Repeal Is Voted Down"

Bennington Review: "After Carrie Kinsey's Letter to Theodore Roosevelt"

BOAAT: "A Face," "Intake Interview," and parts of "The Angel of the Body" and "The Fall / The Tyrant Beetle at the Banks of the Living River of the Dead"

Boston Review: "The Role of the Negro in the Work of Art"

Catch Up: "I Fight Him (Ann Parker)"

Denver Quarterly: "Awaiting the Guns" and "Seawhere"

Free Verse: "Display Food"

The Iowa Review: "The Brown Horse Ariel," "Guns Will Be Guns," and "The President Visits the Storm"

Love's Executive Order: "Everything I Know About Blackness I

Learned from Donald Trump" and "Sonnet for Desiree
Fairooz Prosecuted for Laughing at Jeff Sessions' Confirma⁄
tion Hearing"

LVNG: Parts of "A Glimpse of the Burning Edge of Heaven,"
"The Angel of the Body," and "The Fall / The Tyrant Beetle
at the Banks of the Living River of the Dead"

Plume: "The Monster Made of America Dreams of America"

Surface: "After a Photograph of a Town House in the Lafayette
Park Residential District Detroit"

Tin House: "Remembering My White Grandmother Who Loved
Me and Hated Everybody Like Me"

The Yale Review: "Hatred"

"We'll Go No More a Roving" was originally published in *Poems for Political Disaster*, and was reprinted in *The New York Times*.

"Shane McCrae is a shrewd composer of American stories . . . He is a prospector for speech rhythms, collecting his material wherever he can. But American attics are full of old boxes of diaries and letters; and testimony, no matter how arresting, is not itself poetry. What makes McCrae's compositions so ingenious is their marvels of prosody and form, learned from the English Renaissance poems that he read in libraries when he was just starting out. The result is beautifully up-to-date, old-fashioned work, where the dignity of English meters meets, as in a mosh pit, the vitality—and often the brutality—of American speech."
—DAN CHIASSON, *The New Yorker*

In *The Gilded Auction Block*, the acclaimed poet Shane McCrae considers the present moment in America on its own terms as well as for what it says about the American project and Americans themselves. In the book's four sections, McCrae alternately responds directly to Donald Trump and contextualizes him historically and personally, exploding the illusions of freedom of both black and white Americans. A moving, incisive, and frightening exploration of both the legacy and the current state of white supremacy in this country, *The Gilded Auction Block* is a book about the present that reaches into the past and stretches toward the future.

"Shane McCrae has many gifts as a poet, but among his most hypnotizing is his ability to create poems that simultaneously blare and beacon . . . McCrae has been creating ambitious work that demands—earns—our attention. I often feel out of time when I am reading his words; they arrive with a Miltonic fury, and yet they are so contemporary and critical for our present, strange world."
—NICK RIPATRAZONE, *The Millions*

SHANE McCRAE is the author of five previous books of poetry: *In the Language of My Captor*, which won the Anisfield-Wolf Book Award for Poetry and was a finalist for the National Book Award, the Los Angeles Times Book Prize, and the William Carlos Williams Award; *The Animal Too Big to Kill*, winner of the 2014 Lexi Rudnitsky Editor's Choice Award; *Forgiveness Forgiveness*; *Blood*; and *Mule*. He is the recipient of a Whiting Award, a National Endowment for the Arts Fellowship, a Lannan Literary Award, and a Guggenheim Fellowship. He teaches at Columbia University and lives in New York City.

COVER DESIGN by Quemadura
COVER ART from *Monstrorum Historia* (History of Monsters), 1642, by Ulisse Aldrovandi

FARRAR, STRAUS AND GIROUX
WWW.FSGBOOKS.COM

Poetry
$16.00 / $22.00 Can.
ISBN: 978-0-374-53871-2

51600 >

9 780374 538712